EMPIRES IN THE MIDDLE AGES

THE OTTOMAN EMPIRE

EDITED BY
CAROLYN DECARLO

Britannica·
Educational Publishing

IN ASSOCIATION WITH

ROSEN
EDUCATIONAL SERVICES

T0405593

Published in 2018 by Britannica Educational Publishing (a trademark of Encyclopædia Britannica, Inc.) in association with The Rosen Publishing Group, Inc. 29 East 21st Street, New York, NY 10010

Copyright © 2018 by Encyclopædia Britannica, Inc. Britannica, Encyclopædia Britannica, and the Thistle logo are registered trademarks of Encyclopædia Britannica, Inc. All rights reserved.

Rosen Publishing materials copyright © 2018 The Rosen Publishing Group, Inc. All rights reserved.

Distributed exclusively by Rosen Publishing.
To see additional Britannica Educational Publishing titles, go to rosenpublishing.com.

First Edition

Britannica Educational Publishing
J.E. Luebering: Executive Director, Core Editorial
Andrea R. Field: Managing Editor, Compton's by Britannica

Rosen Publishing
Carolyn DeCarlo: Editor
Nelson Sá: Art Director
Brian Garvey: Designer
Cindy Reiman: Photography Manager
Nicole DiMella: Photo Researcher

Library of Congress Cataloging-in-Publication Data

Names: DeCarlo, Carolyn, editor.
Title: The Ottoman Empire / edited by Carolyn DeCarlo.
Description: New York : Britannica Educational Publishing, in Association with Rosen Educational Services, 2018. | Series: Empires in the Middle Ages | Audience: Grades 5–8. | Includes bibliographical references and index.
Identifiers: LCCN 2017021551| ISBN 9781680487855 (library bound) | ISBN 9781680488685 (paperback) | ISBN 9781680488692 (6 pack)
Subjects: LCSH: Turkey—History—Ottoman Empire, 1288–1918—Juvenile literature.
Classification: LCC DR486 .D29 2018 | DDC 956/.015—dc23
LC record available at https://lccn.loc.gov/201702155

Manufactured in China

Photo credits: Cover Heritage Images/Hulton Fine Art Collection/Getty Images; pp. 5, 6, 40 © Encyclopædia Britannica, Inc.; p. 7 DEA Picture Library/De Agostini/Getty Images; p. 10 © Courtesy of Istanbul University Library; p. 12 © Roland Michaud-Rapho/Photo Researchers; p. 13 Pantheon/SuperStock; pp. 15, 23 Leemage /Universal Images Group/Getty Images;
p. 17 Universal History Archive/Universal Images Group/Getty Images; p. 18 © Los Angeles County Museum of Art, The Edwin Binney, 3rd, Collection of Turkish Art at the Los Angeles County Museum of Art (M.85.237.42), www.lacma.org; p. 20 © William J. Bowe; pp. 25, 38 © Sonia Halliday; p. 27 © Courtesy of the trustees of the British Museum; pp. 28–29 Topkapi Palace Museum, Istanbul, Turkey/Sonia Halliday Photographs/Bridgeman Images; p. 30 Michael Nicholson/Corbis Historical/ Getty Images; p. 33 © Ann Hill/Sonia Halliday Photographs; pp. 34–35 © Photos.com/Jupiterimages; p. 36 © Los Angeles County Museum of Art, The Edwin Binney, 3rd, Collection of Turkish Art at the Los Angeles County Museum of Art (M.85.237.47), www.lacma.org; p. 41 © George Grantham Bain Collection/Library of Congress, Washington D.C. (Digital File Number: cph 3b24436).

CONTENTS

E arly in the fourteenth century, a Turkish tribal chieftain named Osman founded an empire in Asia Minor that continued for almost six hundred years. From its center in what is now western Turkey, the Ottoman Empire, as it came to be known, grew by conquering the Byzantine Empire and lands beyond. It included at its height all of Asia Minor and most of southeastern Europe, portions of the Middle East, North Africa as far west as Algeria, and large parts of the Arabian Peninsula.

Osman's ancestors were bands of horsemen who invaded Asia Minor in the eleventh century from the Central Asian land of Turkistan. Among these tribes were the Seljuks, who established a small state in Asia Minor called the sultanate of Rum (Rome). The Seljuks attacked the Arabs in Syria and Palestine. Recent converts to Islam, they also fought against the Christian Byzantine state, which occupied much of Asia Minor and lands to the west, including Greece. In 1071, Seljuk warriors defeated the Byzantine emperor Romanus IV at Manzikert and took him prisoner. In the same year, they conquered Jerusalem— and with it, the Holy Land.

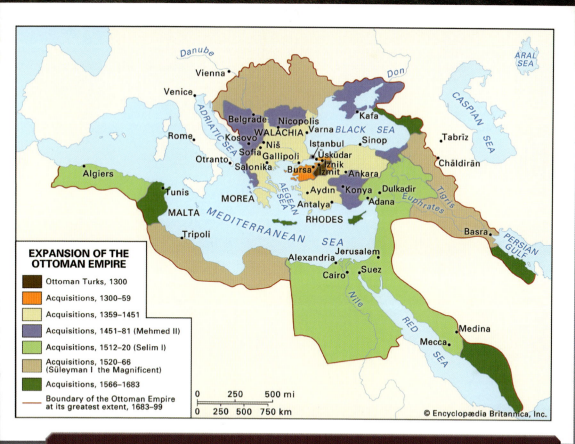

This map shows the expansion of the Ottoman Empire (1300–1699).

The Byzantines held most of Asia Minor and their capital at Constantinople (now Istanbul), appealing to the pope in Rome for help. For the next two centuries, the Christians of Europe fought the Seljuk Turks in seven Crusades. The Seljuks stood their ground throughout the holy wars, only to then be attacked by new assailants from Central Asia. Among the leaders of the invasion was Osman, who established the dynasty that would carry his name, as Ottoman, across history.

Expansion characterized the first two hundred years of Ottoman rule, as Ottoman control spread

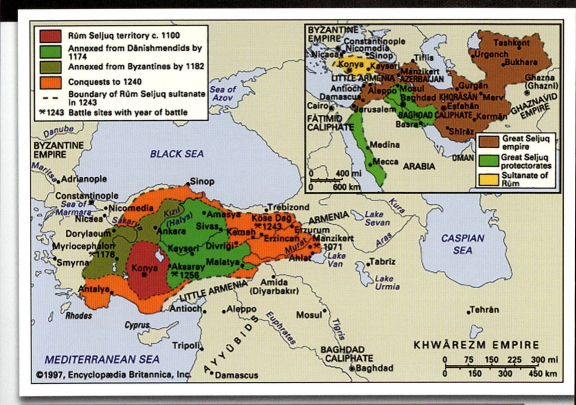

A map shows the Rum sultanate, with an inset of the Seljuk empire, circa 1080.

across all of Asia Minor and most of southeastern Europe. During the sixteenth century, new conquests extended the empire's domain into central Europe and the Middle East. Under Suleyman I (ruled 1520–66), the empire achieved a degree of wealth, power, and grandeur unparalleled in Ottoman history. The customs and societies of the conquered Islamic empires merged with those inherited from Byzantium and the great Turkish empires of Central Asia, reestablishing themselves in forms that persisted throughout the Ottoman Empire and into modern times.

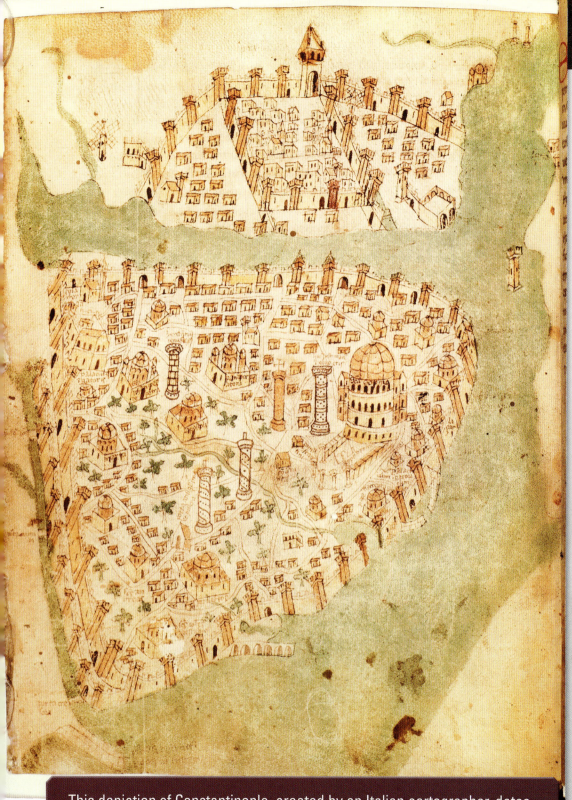

This depiction of Constantinople, created by an Italian cartographer, dates to the fifteenth century after the city was captured by the Ottoman Turks.

But changes during Suleyman's reign brought the start of a slow and steady decline. Following his death, the military took control of the government, diminishing the power of the sultanate. As the central government weakened, many regions in the empire began to act independently, displaying minimal loyalty to the sultan and the state. The empire's weakness was met with a West growing in power and assertiveness. Ottoman wars with Venice and Vienna in the late seventeenth century preceded decades of conflicts with other European nation-states, leading to great losses of territory. Russia waged several wars against the empire in the nineteenth century, gaining control of the Black Sea. The Ottomans survived the Crimean War (1854–56) and the Russo-Turkish War (1877–78) largely with the aid of Western powers, including Great Britain, France, and Sardinia.

By the early twentieth century, the empire was on the brink of collapse. Siding with Germany in World War I, the empire failed to hold Constantinople and several other strategic areas. By 1920, the Ottomans had signed the Treaty of Sèvres, which abolished the Ottoman Empire and all rights over its territories in the Middle East and North Africa. The Treaty of Lausanne (1923) established the boundaries of the modern state of Turkey. The six-hundred-year reign of the Ottoman Empire had come to an end.

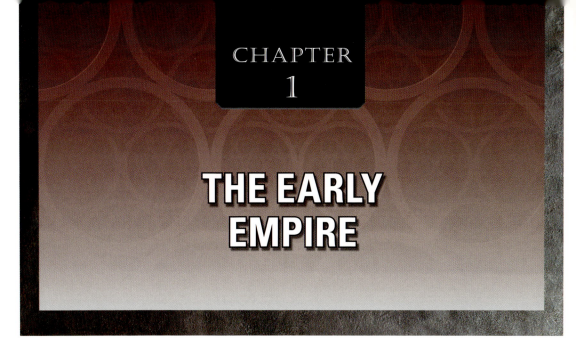

THE EARLY EMPIRE

The Ottoman Empire began about 1300 CE when the family of the Turkish warrior Osman gained a foothold in Asia Minor (also called Anatolia), the peninsula of land that today constitutes the Asian part of Turkey. The Osmans established a principality that spread from a small area in northwestern Asia Minor to cover most of the Anatolian Peninsula and much of southeastern Europe. At its peak, the empire also included large swaths of the Middle East, North Africa, and the Arabian Peninsula. The dynasty that Osman founded was called Osmanli, meaning "sons of Osman." Both the name of the dynasty and the empire it established are derived from Uthman, the Arabic form of his name.

OSMAN AND HIS SUCCESSORS

During the eleventh century, bands of nomadic Turks emerged from their home in Central Asia to raid lands

Osman I is featured in a miniature from a sixteenth-century manuscript illustrating the dynasty.

to the west. A fierce group called the Seljuk Turks soon established themselves in Iran and Mesopotamia, growing to occupy much of Asia Minor during the twelfth century. The Seljuks fought against the Byzantine Christians as well as warriors from the Mongol Empire, who invaded Asia Minor in the thirteenth century. After defeating the Seljuks in 1293, the Mongols controlled much of eastern Asia Minor; the remainder was occupied by several independent Turkmen principalities—the strongest of which was led by Osman in the northwest.

The initial areas of expansion under Osman I and his successors—Orhan (ruled 1326–59) and Murad I (ruled 1359–89)—were western Asia Minor and southeastern Europe, primarily the Balkan Peninsula. As the major Muslim rivals of Byzantium, the Ottomans attracted masses of nomads and unemployed city dwellers who were searching for a way to earn a living and also seeking to fulfill their religious desire to expand the territory of Islam.

Orhan's capture of several key cities allowed him to expand the Ottoman holdings into a real state and create an army, which he filled with Christian mercenary troops. Ottoman raiding parties began to move regularly into Thrace, a region to the northwest of Constantinople that includes parts of Turkey, Bulgaria, and Greece. Huge quantities of captured treasure strengthened Ottoman power and attracted thousands of the uprooted people of Asia Minor into Ottoman service.

MURAD I IN ADRIANOPLE

Orhan's son Murad I conquered Thrace in 1361. He moved his capital to Adrianople (now Edirne), Thrace's capital and a key city of the Byzantine Empire. This conquest effectively cut off Constantinople from the outside world. Adrianople also controlled the principal invasion route through the Balkan Mountains, giving the Ottomans access to further expansion to the north.

From there, Murad moved into Bulgaria, capturing the city of Philippopolis (now Plovdiv) in 1363. This brought the Ottomans control of critical grain and tax

The mosque of Bayezid (1506) is a prominent feature in Edirne, Turkey—formerly known as Adrianople, capital of Thrace and the early Ottoman Empire.

revenues. The Byzantine emperor John V Palaeologus tried to mobilize European assistance by uniting the churches of Constantinople and Rome, but that effort only further divided Byzantium without assuring any concrete help from the West.

Murad worked to incorporate European land-owners into his rapidly expanding empire. He retained local native rulers, who in return accepted his rule, paid annual tributes, and provided soldiers for his army when required. The policy of keeping the local rulers in place enabled the Ottomans to avoid resistance by assuring the local rulers and their subjects that their lives, properties, traditions, and positions would be preserved if they peacefully accepted Ottoman rule. It also allowed the Ottomans to govern the newly conquered areas without building up a vast administrative system of their own or maintaining an army of occupation.

To consolidate his empire in the Balkans, Murad began a series of battles against the Balkan states in 1371, capturing Macedonia, central Bulgaria, and Ser-

Murad I, sultan of the Ottoman Empire, was killed in the Battle of Kosovo while fighting the Serbs and Bosnians in 1389.

bia. He was killed during the climactic defeat of the Balkan allies at the Battle of Kosovo in 1389.

BAYEZID I AND TIMUR LENK

Murad I was succeeded by his son Bayezid I (ruled 1389–1402). In the early years of Bayezid's reign, Ottoman forces conducted campaigns that succeeded in controlling vast Balkan territories. He then turned his attention to threats posed by various Turkish rulers in Asia Minor. He annexed several Anatolian principalities, defeating the critical principality of Karaman in 1397.

Bayezid's successes attracted the attention of Timur Lenk, a Mongolian conqueror who had been building a powerful empire in Central Asia, Iran, Afghanistan, and Mesopotamia. Encouraged by Turkish princes who had fled to his court from Bayezid's incursions, Timur decided to destroy Bayezid's empire before turning his attentions back to the east. He invaded Asia Minor and overwhelmed Bayezid and his army in 1402. Taken captive by Timur, Bayezid died within a year.

Timur's objective in Asia Minor had not been conquest, but rather to secure a western boundary that would enable him to make further conquests in the east. He left Asia Minor greatly divided—some areas were restored to the Turkish princes who had supported him, whereas large parts of western Asia Minor and south-

This portrait of Bayezid I was included in a miniature from the *Zubdat al-Tawarikh* (Cream of histories) dedicated to Sultan Murad III in 1583.

western Europe remained under Ottoman control.

DIVISIONS AND CONQUESTS

Internal divisions within the empire hindered Ottoman efforts to restore their power during a period that came to be known as the Interregnum (1402–13). During this period, four of Bayezid's sons competed for the right to rule the entire empire. The sons fought for the throne until one, Mehmed I, killed the other three and took control. Mehmed I reigned from 1413 to 1421 and his successor, Murad II, from 1421 to 1451. Their rule marked a new period of expansion in which Bayezid's empire was restored and new territories were added.

Mehmed I reunified the divided Ottoman territories, consolidating Ottoman control in much of Asia Minor. He pursued a policy of relative restraint in the Balkans, although he extended his control into Albania and conducted raids into Hungary. Murad II expanded Ottoman rule in the Balkans and helped lead the empire toward the path of full recovery.

The task of finishing the Balkan conquests and seizing all of Asia Minor, however, fell to Murad's successor, Mehmed II (ruled 1451–81). A great military leader, Mehmed II captured Constantinople in 1453 and made it the capital of the Ottoman Empire. He then set out to conquer the territories that would form the Ottoman Empire's heartland for the next four centu-

Sultan Mehmed II is shown smelling a rose in this miniature from the *Sarayi Albums*, circa 1480, kept in the Topkapi Palace.

THE JANISSARIES

Starting in the late fourteenth century, the Ottomans began to develop an elite military force made up of Christian recruits who were converted to Islam. The recruits gained the knowledge and experience needed to serve in the government as well as the

A Turkish manuscript illustration depicts Osman II in a procession of Janissaries and guards, circa 1620–22.

infantry branch of the military. The corps, known as the Janissaries, served as the standing army of the Ottoman Empire until 1826.

The recruits were taken for life service between the ages of ten and twenty, usually from the Balkan provinces. Though members were well paid and educated, separation from family and home was harsh; the men were subject to strict rules and not allowed to marry. In the late sixteenth century, many of these restrictions were relaxed.

Highly respected for their military prowess, the Janissaries became a powerful political force within the Ottoman state, and frequently engineered palace coups. Their end came in June 1826 in the so-called Auspicious Incident. On learning of the formation of new, westernized troops, the Janissaries revolted. Sultan Mahmud II (ruled 1808–1839) declared war on the newly-minted "rebels." Most of the Janissaries were killed in the attack, and those who were taken prisoner were executed.

ries. All of Asia Minor was secured, as were the entire Balkan Peninsula south of Hungary, the Crimean Peninsula, and parts of southern Italy.

REPAIRING CONSTANTINOPLE

Mehmed II worked to consolidate his expanding empire and to restore Constantinople as a great political, economic, and social center. Special attention was paid to restoring Constantinople's industry and trade, with substantial concessions made to attract merchants and artisans. Old buildings were repaired;

The Rumeli Fortress was built on the bank of the Bosporus River in 1452, during Mehmed II's restoration of Constantinople (now Istanbul, Turkey).

streets, aqueducts, and bridges were constructed; sanitary facilities were modernized; and a vast supply system was established to provide for the city's inhabitants. After converting the Byzantine-era church of Hagia Sophia into a mosque, Mehmed established charitable foundations and provided generously each year for the mosque's upkeep.

Mehmed advocated growth of the city with not only its former inhabitants but also many of the conquered peoples of the empire. Their residence and intermingling in Constantinople became a model for a powerful and integrated empire. Thousands of Christians and Muslims were brought to the city, as were Jews from central and western Europe. The major religious groups were allowed to establish their own self-governing communities, called *millets*. Each millet carried out social and administrative functions not assumed by the Ottoman ruling class, including the retention of its own religious laws, traditions, and language.

Many historians consider Mehmed II the most broad-minded and freethinking of the Ottoman sultans, elevating mathematics, astronomy, and Muslim theology to their highest level. He gathered Italian and Greek scholars at his court and collected a library of their works. He erected eight highly regarded colleges of Islamic sciences, and assembled learned Muslim teachers so that they might discuss theological problems in his presence. Mehmed himself left behind a *divan*, a collection of poems in the traditional style of classical Ottoman literature.

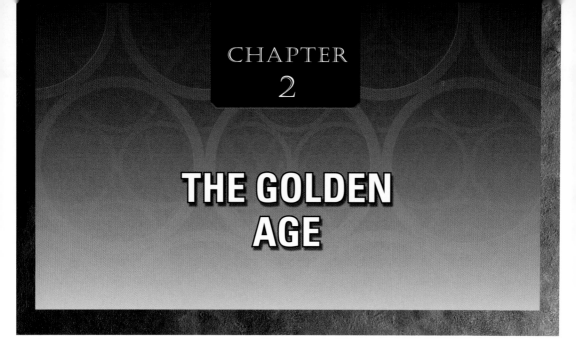

CHAPTER 2

THE GOLDEN AGE

During the century that followed the reign of Mehmed II, the Ottoman Empire achieved the peak of its power and wealth. New conquests extended its domain well into central Europe and throughout much of North Africa and the Middle East. Three sultans ruled the Ottoman Empire at its height: Bayezid II, Selim I, and Suleyman I the Magnificent.

BAYEZID II: PACIFIST AND MYSTIC

The reign of Mehmed II's immediate successor, Bayezid II (ruled 1481–1512), was largely a period of rest. Previous conquests were consolidated, and many of the political, economic, and social problems caused by Mehmed's internal policies were resolved.

At home, Bayezid restored most of the property confiscated by his father from military campaigns to its original owners. Equal taxes were established

A portrait of Bayezid II from the *Zubdat al-Tawarikh* (Cream of histories), dedicated to Sultan Murad III in 1583.

around the empire so that all subjects could fulfill their obligations to the government. To help expand the economy, immigration was welcomed. Among the newcomers were thousands of Jews who had been expelled from Spain by the Inquisition during the summer of 1492. They settled particularly in Constantinople, Salonika (present-day Thessaloniki, Greece), and Edirne, joining the Jews who already lived there in a golden age of Ottoman Jewry that lasted well into the seventeenth century.

Abroad, Bayezid extended the empire in Europe by adding outposts along the Black Sea. He turned the Ottoman fleet into a major Mediterranean naval power. Late in life, Bayezid became a religious mystic. He brought mystic rituals and teachings into the institutions and practices of orthodox Islam. In the end, Bayezid's increasingly mystic and peaceful nature led the Janissaries to dethrone him in favor of his militant son Selim I.

SELIM I: MASTER ACHIEVER

Selim's first task as ruler was to eliminate all competition for his position. His method was ruthless: he had his brothers, their sons, and all but one of his own sons killed. He took control of the army, which had wanted to raise its own candidate to power. During his reign (1512–20), the Ottomans moved into Syria, Arabia, and Egypt, thereby doubling the size of the empire.

Selim I is featured in this detail from a sixteenth-century miniature kept in the Topkapi Palace Museum, Istanbul.

By acquiring the holy places of Islam, Selim cemented his position as the religion's most powerful ruler. This gave the Ottomans direct access to the rich cultural heritage of the Arab world. Leading Muslim intellectuals, artists, artisans, and administrators came to Constantinople from all parts of the Arab world. They made the empire much more of a traditional Islamic state than it had been. A leading representative of Mecca presented Selim with the keys to that holy city, a symbolic gesture acknowledging Selim as the leader of the Muslim world.

An added benefit of Selim's efforts was control of all Middle Eastern trade routes between Europe and East Asia. The growth of the empire had for some time been an impediment to European trade. In time this led European states to seek routes around Africa to China and India. It also impelled them to face westward, and led directly to the European discovery of the Americas.

SULEYMAN I THE MAGNIFICENT

Selim's last years were spent in Constantinople solidifying the supremacy of the sultanate. During the long reign of his surviving son and successor, Suleyman I (ruled 1520–66), the foundations laid by Selim were used to establish the classical Ottoman state and society, and to make important new conquests in the East and West.

Suleyman I the Magnificent rides on horseback during a procession through Constantinople in this engraving of a panel, circa 1533.

Suleyman I—called "the Magnificent" in Europe and "the Lawgiver" among the Ottomans—came to the throne in an enviable situation. He had no opposition and enjoyed considerable control over the military, as well as over the remnants of the Turkish nobility. As a result of his father's conquests, new revenues from the expanded empire left him with wealth and power unparalleled in Ottoman history. His reign marked the peak of Ottoman grandeur and is regarded as the golden age of Ottoman history.

In his early campaigns, Suleyman scored military victories over the Christian powers in the Mediterranean region and central Europe. His armies conquered Belgrade in 1521, Rhodes in 1522, and the powerful Hungarian stronghold at Mohács on the Danube River in 1526. He laid siege to Vienna in 1529 but was soon forced to withdraw. Pressing on, he gained control of key regions in Persia and conquered Iraq.

Organized military conflict shifted to the sea, with the Ottomans emerging for the first time as a major naval power. Suleyman made Khayr al-Din (known to Europeans as "Barbarossa") the grand admiral of the Ottoman naval forces. Khayr al-Din was a Turkish captain who had built a major pirate fleet of

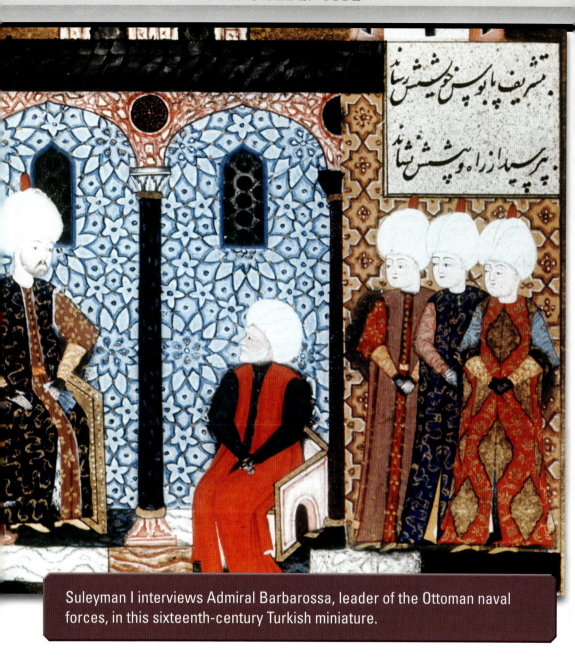

Suleyman I interviews Admiral Barbarossa, leader of the Ottoman naval forces, in this sixteenth-century Turkish miniature.

sea ghazis (raiders) in the western Mediterranean. In service to the Ottomans, he used his expertise to capture Algiers, Tripoli, and other North African ports.

29

TURKS AT SEA

Barbarossa (Italian for "Redbeard") was the name given to Khayr al-Din, a Barbary pirate who became chief admiral of the Ottoman fleet and by whose initiative Algeria and Tunisia became part of the Ottoman Empire. For three centuries after his death, Mediterranean coastal towns and villages were ravaged by his pirate successors.

Born Khidr, Barbarossa was one of four sons of a Turk from the island of Lesbos. Hatred of the Spanish and Portuguese who attacked North Africa between 1505 and 1511 encouraged Khidr and his brother Aruj to intensify their piracy. They hoped, with the aid of Turks and Muslim emigrants from Spain, to wrest an African domain

This portrait of Khayr al-Din aptly includes a depiction of a naval battle, as the man who became known as Admiral Barbarossa was first a successful Barbary pirate.

for themselves. However, just as their plan began to succeed, Aruj was killed by the Spanish in 1518. Khidr, who had been his brother's lieutenant, then assumed the title Khayr al-Din. Fearing he would lose his possessions to the Spanish, he offered homage to the Ottoman sultan. In return, he was granted the high title *beylerbey* and sent military reinforcements. With that aid, Khayr al-Din was able to capture Algiers in 1529 and make it a great stronghold of Mediterranean piracy.

Khayr al-Din was appointed admiral-in-chief of the Ottoman Empire in 1533. The next year, he conquered the whole of Tunisia for the Turks, with the city of Tunis itself becoming the base of piracy against the Italian coast. The Holy Roman emperor Charles V led a Crusade that captured Tunis and Goletta in 1535, but Barbarossa defeated Charles V's fleet three years later at the Battle of Preveza, securing the eastern Mediterranean for the Turks. Barbarossa remained one of the great figures of the court at Constantinople until his death in 1546.

In more peaceful pursuits, Suleyman adorned the chief cities of the Islamic world with mosques, aqueducts, bridges, and other public works. In Constantinople, he commissioned the great Ottoman architect Sinan to build several mosques, including the Sehzade Mosque and the magnificent Mosque of Suleyman. The nonruling class prospered socially under Suleyman's expansion of the millet system, and the various guilds (associations of craftspeople) offered the populace economic prosperity.

IMPERIAL DECLINE AND FALL

The Ottoman Empire under Suleyman reached the height of its political power and brought increased territory under Ottoman control. The seeds of decline, however, were already planted. Factoring greatly in this decline was the decreasing influence of the sultans themselves.

A SHIFT IN AUTHORITY

Having reached the heights of power and wealth, Suleyman grew tired of military campaigns and the duties of governing. He gradually withdrew from public affairs, preferring instead the privacy of his harem. To take his place, the office of grand vizier was expanded to become second only to the sultan in authority and revenue. The grand vizier's authority included the right to demand and obtain absolute obedience. While the grand vizier was able to stand in for the sultan in official functions, he could not take his place as the focus of loyalty for all classes and groups in the empire. This separation of political loyalty and central authority led to a decline in the government's ability to impose its will on the people.

Named for the town in western Asia Minor where they were made, these Iznik earthenware wall tiles adorned the harem of the Topkapi Palace during the sixteenth century.

After the death of Suleyman in 1566, the army gained control of the sultanate and was able to use it for its own benefit. The army seized taxable land from the notables, transforming it into great private estates—depriving the state of services as well as revenue. In this way, the Janissaries and the associated artillery corps became the most important segments of the Ottoman army.

Few sultans after Suleyman had the ability to exercise real power when the need arose. Power fell first into the hands of the women of the harem, during the "Sultanate of the Women" (1570–78), and then into the grasp of the chief Janissary officers, who dominated from 1578 to 1625. Anarchy slowly increased throughout the empire, leading to the fracture of Ottoman society into separate and increasingly hostile communities.

SEA POWER FROM THE WEST

The weakness at home was countered by a growing power in the West. The nation-states of Europe were emerging from the Middle Ages under strong monarchies. They were building armies and navies that were powerful enough to attack the decaying Ottoman military might. In 1571, the combined fleets of Venice, Spain, and the Papal States of Italy defeated the Ottoman navy in the great battle of Lepanto, off the coast of Greece. This defeat took place during the reign of Selim II (ruled 1566–74), the son and heir of Suleyman I. The Ottoman Empire rebuilt its navy, however, and continued to control the eastern Mediterranean for another century.

As the central government became weaker, large parts of the empire began to act independently, retaining only nominal loyalty to the sultan. The army was still strong enough, however, to prevent provincial rebels from asserting complete control. Under Murad III (ruled 1574–95) new campaigns were undertaken. The Caucasus was conquered, and Azerbaijan was seized. This brought the empire to the peak of its territorial extent.

Reform efforts undertaken by seventeenth-century sultans did little to deter the onset of decay. The Ottomans were driven out of the Caucasus and Azerbaijan in 1603 and out of Iraq in 1604. Iraq was retaken by Murad IV (ruled 1623–40) in 1638, but Iran

The battle of Lepanto, October 7, 1571, in which the allied forces of Spain, Venice, and the Papal States defeated the Ottoman Turks, marked the first significant victory for a Christian naval force over a Turkish fleet.

remained a persistent military threat in the east. A long war with Venice (1645–69) exposed Constantinople to an attack by the Venetian navy. In 1683, the last attempt to conquer Vienna failed. Russia and Austria fought the Ottomans by direct military attack and by inciting revolt by non-Muslim subjects of the sultan.

Beginning in 1683 with the attack on Vienna, the Ottomans were at war with European enemies for the next four decades. As a result, the empire lost much of its Balkan territory and all of its possessions on the

THE TULIP PERIOD

Beginning in the early eighteenth century, some Ottomans under the influence of the grand vizier Ibrahim Pasa began to dress like Europeans, and the palace began to imitate European court life. Sultan Ahmed III (ruled 1703–30) built several lavish summer residences near the Bosporus Strait. Members of Ahmed's immediate entourage built similarly lavish houses, holding frequent garden parties in imitation of the pleasures of Versailles in France. The sultan and his ministers were no longer confined behind the walls of the Topkapi palace in Constantinople. The new era, which extended from 1717 to 1730, was a time of

This delicate ink and watercolor painting of a tulip dates to the early eighteenth century in Turkey, during what is now known as the Tulip Period.

peace and deep appreciation of the arts. It came to be known as the Tulip Period.

The period took its name from the widespread practice of growing tulips. Cultivation of the flower signified Westernization to the people, and it became an obsession with rich and poor alike. This was celebrated by the court poet Nedim, whose poetry demonstrates a considerable awareness of his environment and an appreciation of nature. In 1727, Turkish-language books were printed for the first time in the empire. Though the press was closed at times, during the remainder of the century it provided a number of books on history and geography that further opened the minds of the literate.

shores of the Black Sea. In addition, the Austrians and Russians were allowed to intervene in the empire's affairs on behalf of the sultan's Christian subjects.

RULERS IN THE PROVINCES

The weakness of the central government, as manifested by its military decline, also showed itself in a gradual loss of control over most of the provinces. Local notables carved for themselves permanent regions in which they ruled directly, regardless of the wishes of the sultan in Constantinople. The notables were able to build their power bases because they knew of the sultan's military weakness and because local populations preferred their rule to the corrupt administration of the faraway capital. The notables formed their own armies and collected their own taxes, sending only nominal contributions to the imperial treasury.

LAST ATTEMPTS AT REFORM

Selim III (ruled 1789–1807) attempted to reform the empire's treasury and its Janissary corps, creating a new European-style army using modern weapons and tactics. The older military corps, however, remained intact and hostile to the new force, and Selim was overthrown. When Mahmud II (ruled 1808–39) came to the throne, the empire was in desperate straits. Control of North Africa had passed to local notables. In Egypt, the high-ranking governor Muhammad Ali challenged the sultan with the hope of securing greater independence for Egypt. However, his efforts brought the

This detail from a portrait of Selim III is kept in the Topkapi Palace Museum, Istanbul.

intervention of European powers that backed the sultan. Had the Europeans cooperated with Ali, together they could have destroyed the Ottoman Empire.

In 1826, five years after Greece began its fight for independence, the Janissaries revolted to stop reforms. Mahmud had them massacred and constructed a European system in the style of his predecessor, Selim. He also reformed the administration and gained control over some of the provincial notables, except in Egypt. By the time of Mahmud's death, the empire was more consolidated and powerful, but it was still subject to European interference.

Mahmud's sons, Abdulmecid I (ruled 1839–61) and Abdulaziz (ruled 1861–76), carried out further reforms, especially in education and law. However, by mid-century it was evident that the Ottoman cause was hopeless. Tsar Nicholas I of Russia commented on the Ottoman Empire in 1853: "We have on our hands a sick man, a very sick man."

EUROPE ON THE DOORSTEP

The conflicting interests of European states propped up the Ottoman Empire until after World War I. Great Britain especially was determined to keep Russia from gaining direct access to the Mediterranean from the Black Sea. Britain, France, and Sardinia helped the Ottomans during the Crimean War (1853–56) to block the Russians.

In the Russo-Turkish War of 1877–78, Russia and Serbia came to the aid of Bosnia and Herzegovina and Bulgaria in their rebellions against Turkish rule. The Russians took Adrianople and almost reached Constantinople. The Ottomans were forced to sign the harsh Treaty of San Stefano, which would have ended their rule in Europe. However, Britain and Austria-Hungary, alarmed by the Russian gains contained in the treaty, called the Congress of Berlin, which limited Russia's

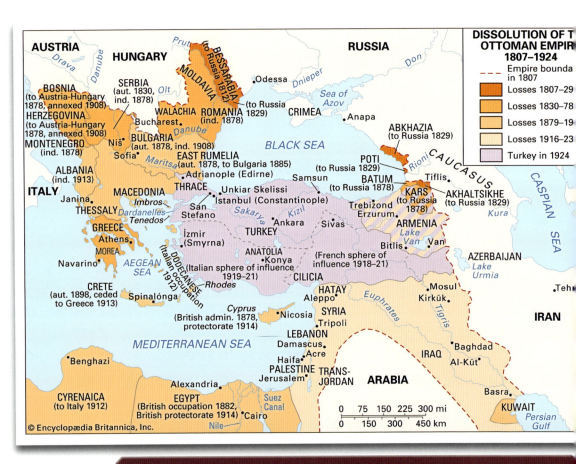

The dissolution of the Ottoman Empire, 1807–1924, is shown.

gains and kept the Ottoman Empire going for a few more decades.

Abdulhamid II (ruled 1876–1909) developed strong ties with Germany, and the Ottomans fought on Germany's side in World War I. German engineers began work on a railway across Turkey that was to link Berlin with Baghdad and the Persian Gulf. Russia hoped to use the war as an excuse to gain access to the Mediterranean and perhaps capture Constantinople. However, the Russian Revolution of 1917 and Russia's subsequent withdrawal from World War I prevented Russia from achieving those goals.

Ottoman defeat in the war inspired an already fervent Turkish nationalism. In 1920, the sultan's representatives signed the Treaty of Sèvres, which abolished the Ottoman Empire and

A photograph of one of the last rulers of the Ottoman Empire, Sultan Adbulhamid II, circa 1890.

obliged Turkey to renounce all rights over Arab Asia and North Africa. The Aegean and Mediterranean coasts were assigned to Greece and Italy, and much of Asia Minor was ceded to the newly created independent state of Armenia.

The postwar settlement outraged the nationalists, however. A new government under the leadership of Mustafa Kemal, known as Ataturk, emerged at Ankara. The last Ottoman sultan, Mehmed VI, fled in 1922 after the sultanate was abolished. The Treaty of Sèvres was replaced in 1923 with the Treaty of Lausanne. Signed by representatives from Turkey and the allied forces of World War I, the new treaty recognized the boundaries of the modern Turkish state. All members of the Ottoman dynasty were expelled from the country a year later, and Turkey was proclaimed a republic, with Ataturk as its first president.

Ataturk succeeded in restoring to his people pride in their Turkishness, coupled with a new sense of accomplishment as the old empire was brought into the modern world. From the ashes of the mighty Ottoman Empire, Ataturk created a modern state that would grow under his successors into a viable democracy, which continues to flourish today.

anarchy A state of lawlessness or political disorder due to the absence of governmental authority.

Anatolia Land that today forms the Asian portion of Turkey; historically called Asia Minor.

harem A usually secluded house or part of a house allotted to women in some Muslim households; the wives, concubines, female relatives, and servants occupying a harem.

impediment Something that makes it difficult to do or complete something; something that interferes with movement or progress.

imperial Of, relating to, or suggestive of an empire.

militant Aggressively active; combatant.

monarchy A state or country whose form of government is headed by a king or queen.

mystic A person who tries to gain religious or spiritual knowledge through prayer and deep thought; someone who practices mysticism.

nationalism Loyalty and devotion to a nation; a sense of national consciousness exalting one nation above all others, with promotion of its culture and interests as opposed to those of other nations.

notable A person summoned to act as a deliberative body; local ruler.

pacifist Strongly and actively opposed to conflict and especially war.

principality The territory or jurisdiction of a prince.

reform The improvement of something by removing faults or problems.

republic A government with a chief of state who is not a monarch and who in modern times is usually a president; a government in which supreme power resides in a body of citizens entitled to vote and overseen by elected representatives responsible to them and governing according to law.

revenue Money collected by a government (as through taxes).

successor One who follows; especially one who succeeds to a throne, title, estate, or office.

sultan A king or sovereign, especially of a Muslim state.

treasury A place in which stores of wealth are kept; a governmental department in charge of finances and the collection and management of public revenues.

Turkistan The area in Central Asia that today encompasses Kazakhstan, Uzbekistan, Tajikistan, Kyrgystan, and Turkmenistan.

vacuum A state of isolation from outside influences.

vizier A high executive officer of various Muslim countries and especially of the Ottoman Empire.

FOR FURTHER READING

Dwyer, Helen. *The Early Modern World, 1492 to 1783* (Curriculum Connections). Redding, CT: Brown Bear Books, 2010.

Feldman, Ruth Tenzer. *The Fall of Constantinople* (Pivotal Moments in History). Minneapolis, MN: Twenty-First Century Books, 2008.

Flatt, Lizann. *Early Islamic Empires*. St. Catharines, ON, Canada: Crabtree Publishing, 2013.

George, Enzo. *The Middle Ages*. New York, NY: Cavendish Square, 2017.

Greenblatt, Miriam. *Suleyman the Magnificent and the Ottoman Empire* (Rulers and Their Times). New York, NY: Benchmark Books, 2003.

Kotapish, Dawn. *Daily Life in Ancient and Modern Baghdad* (Cities Through Time). Minneapolis, MN: Runestone Press, 2000.

Kovacs, Vic. *The Culture of the Islamic World*. New York, NY: Powerkids Press, 2017.

Nagle, Jeanne. *Feudalism, Monarchies, and Nobility* (Political and Economic Systems). New York, NY: Britannica Educational Publishing, 2014.

O'Brian, Pliny. *Empires, Crusaders, and Invasions Through the Middle Ages* (Exploring the Ancient and Medieval Worlds). New York, NY: Cavendish Square, 2015.

Owings, Lisa. *Turkey* (Exploring Countries). Minneapolis, MN: Bellwether Media, 2011.

Rauf, Don. *The Rise and Fall of the Ottoman Empire* (The Rise and Fall of Empires). New York, NY: Rosen Publishing, 2016.

WEBSITES

Because of the changing nature of internet links, Rosen Publishing has developed an online list of websites related to the subject of this book. This site is updated regularly. Please use this link to access this list:

http://www.rosenlinks.com/EIMA/Ottoman